CLONING

SUSAN HENNEBERG

red rhino books®

NONFICTION

Area 51	Monsters of the Deep
Bioweapons	Monsters on Land
Cannibal Animals	Racetracks
Cloning	The Science of Movies
Comet Catcher	Seven Wonders of the
Drones	Ancient World
Fault Lines	3D Printing
Gnarly Sports Injuries	Tuskegee Airmen
Great Spies of the World	Virtual Reality
Hacked	Wild Weather
Little Rock Nine	Witchcraft
Medal of Honor	Wormholes
Military Dogs	Zombie Creatures

SADDLEBACK
EDUCATIONAL PUBLISHING
www.sdlback.com

Photo credits: page 2: jeremy sutton-hibbert / Alamy Stock Photo, Alamy.com; All other source images from Shutterstock.com

ISBN: 978-1-68021-034-7
eBook: 978-1-63078-341-9

Printed in Malaysia

23 22 21 20 19   4 5 6 7 8

TABLE OF CONTENTS

Dolly and Professor Ian Wilmut

Chapter 1
MEET DOLLY

It was 1996.

A group met in Scotland.

They went to a shed.

A lamb was being born.

They all watched.

Why?

This lamb was special.

Most lambs have a mom.

And a dad.

Not this one.

She was a clone.

A copy.

Her name was Dolly.

A sheep is a living animal.
How can it be copied?
It is not easy.
Doctors work with *cells*.
They take *genes* out of one cell.
They put them in a new one.

Things can go wrong.
It took a long time to make Dolly.
277 tries.
She was the first cloned *mammal*.

Most sheep live for 10 years.
Dolly lived only six.
But she was a success.
She made big news.
Cloning took off after that.

Chapter 2
WHAT ARE CLONES?

A *clone* is a copy.
A living copy.
What does this mean?
Think of a plant.
It has a stem.
And roots.
Cut the stem.
New roots grow.
A new plant is made.
Just like the first one.

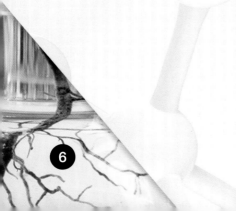

Now think of people.

Some are twins.

Identical twins.

They come from the same cells.

The cells split.

They make two babies.

Each is the same.

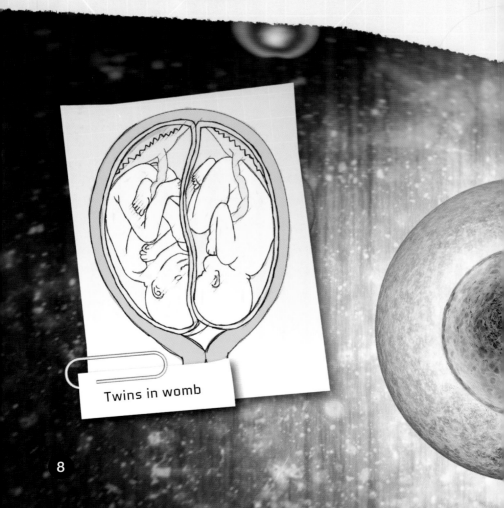

Twins in womb

9

Plants.

Identical twins.

These are *natural* clones.

Think of Dolly.

She was not a natural clone.

People made her in a lab.

She came from one cell.

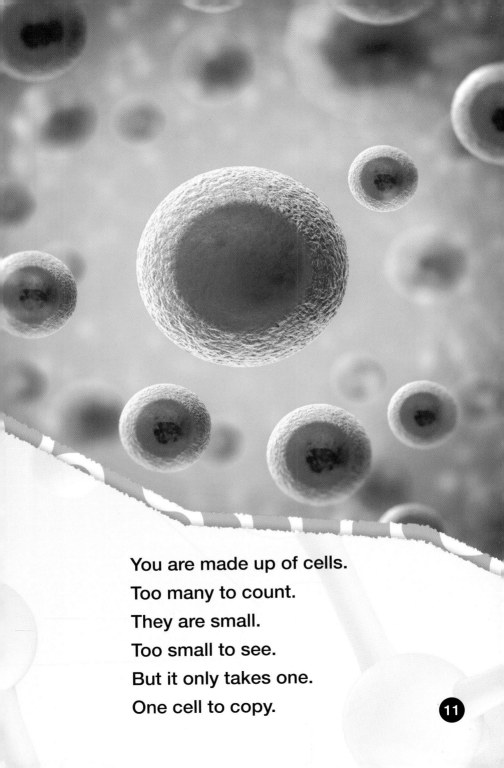

You are made up of cells.

Too many to count.

They are small.

Too small to see.

But it only takes one.

One cell to copy.

Cells have many parts.

One part is the *nucleus*.

It is the cell's brain.

It holds *DNA*.

Genes make up DNA.

They talk to cells.

Tell them how to grow.

Where do you get your genes?

From your parents.

Both of them.

But not clones.

They get genes from one parent.

One cell.

They are copies.

Chapter 3
HISTORY OF CLONING

Cloning cells took time.
100 years.
The first step was in 1902.
Scientists had a salamander.
They took one of its *embryos*.
They split it.
Now there were two.
Two meant two babies.

It was 1952.
Scientists kept trying.
They used frogs.
They tried to copy them.
It worked!
Not many grew.
But it was a step forward.

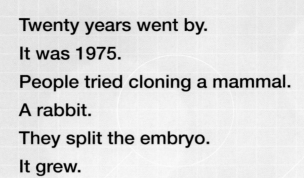

Twenty years went by.

It was 1975.

People tried cloning a mammal.

A rabbit.

They split the embryo.

It grew.

Five years went by.
Sheep were cloned.
Then cows.
Embryos were split.
But none were born.

Then came Dolly.

People heard about her.

More animals were cloned.

Mice.

Monkeys.

Pets.

But no people.

Not yet.

DO YOU COPY?

Scientists cloned a gaur in 2001.
It is a rare ox. It is endangered.
Cloning could help change that.

Chapter 4
HOW TO CLONE

How are clones made?
There are two ways.

One way is *twinning*.
It is done in a lab.
One embryo is used.
It is split into two.
The two grow.
They are put into mothers.
Babies grow from the cells.
They are twins.

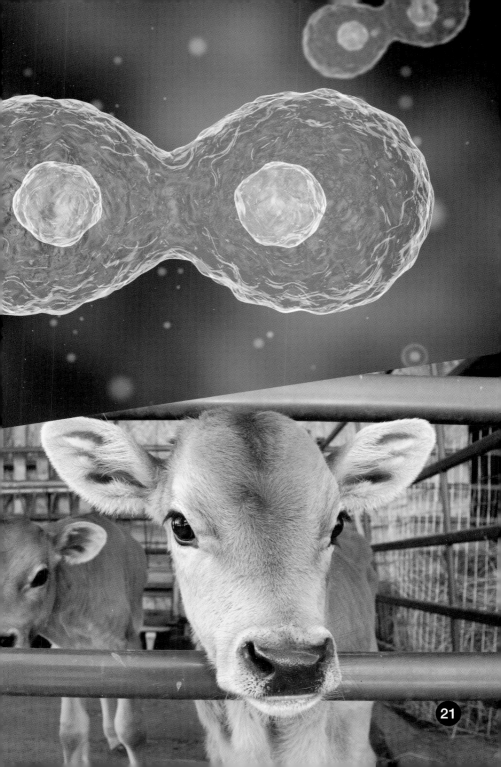

The second way uses cells.
It is also done in a lab.
Somatic cell nuclear *transfer*.
SCNT for short.
Dolly was made this way.
How?

Doctors used two sheep.
They got two cells.
One was a body cell.
The other was an egg cell.
They removed the egg's nucleus.
They put in new DNA.
Where was it from?
The first sheep.
One with different genes.

Somatic Cell Nuclear Transfer Chart

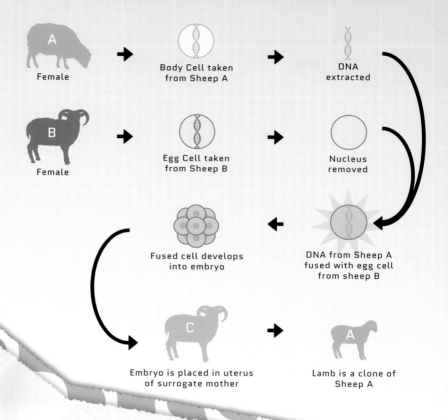

A Female → Body Cell taken from Sheep A → DNA extracted

B Female → Egg Cell taken from Sheep B → Nucleus removed

DNA from Sheep A fused with egg cell from sheep B → Fused cell develops into embryo

Embryo is placed in uterus of surrogate mother → Lamb is a clone of Sheep A

The egg cell split.

It became an embryo.

It was put into a third sheep.

Dolly was born.

Who was her mother?

The first sheep.

Thanks to SCNT.

Chapter 5
CLONING AND TWINS

Identical twins.

They come from the same cells.

The cells split.

They make two babies.

Each is the same.

Or are they?

You may know a twin.

They may look like their brother.

Or sister.

But they are not the same.

DO YOU COPY?

On average, there is one set of identical twins for every 285 pregnancies.

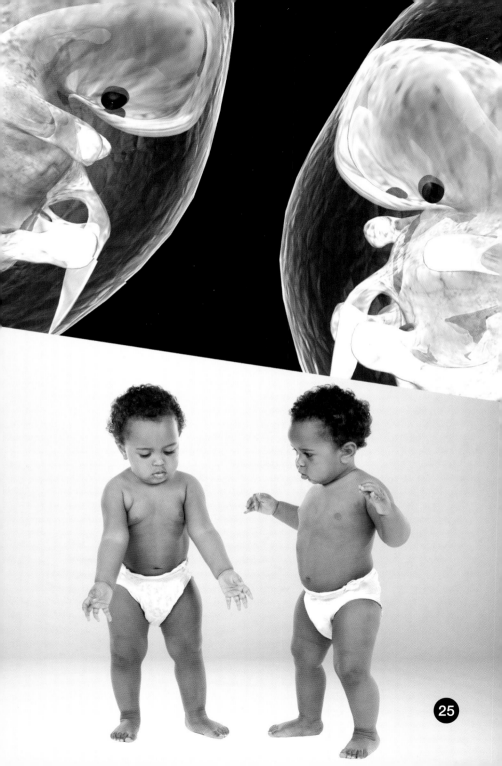

Studies have been done.
They looked at cloned pigs.
They have the same genes.
But they are not exactly the same.
Some are big.
Some are small.
Some have bad lungs.
Others do not.
Tests make it clear.
Copies are not always exact.

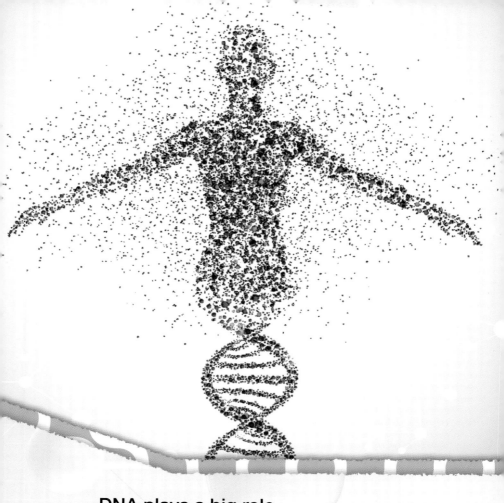

DNA plays a big role.

It affects what we look like.

And how we act.

But things happen to us.

Those things can change us.

Twins share DNA.

But they do not share everything.

They are not exactly alike.

Chapter 6
STEM CELLS

Animals can be cloned.

So can cells.

Cells grow.

They make *tissue*.

Tissue makes up our parts.

Eyes.

Heart.

Skin.

Tissue can be hurt.

A scrape on your knee.

It needs to be fixed.

Your body can do it.

It has repair cells.

Adult *stem cells*.

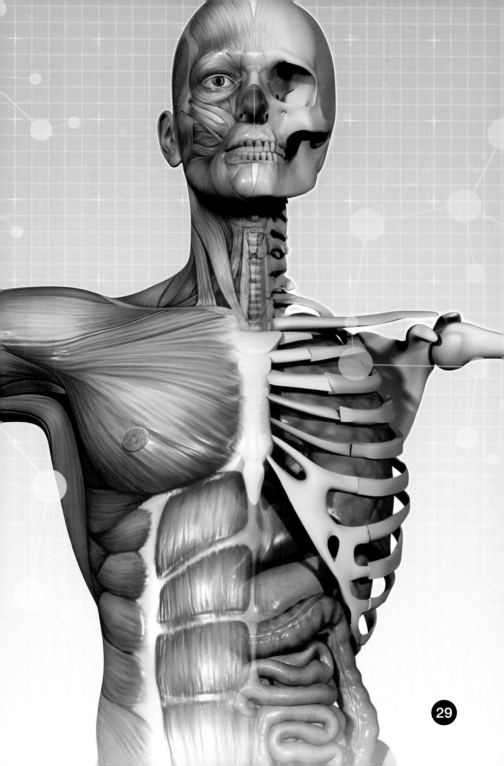

29

You may get a cut.
It may bleed.
Your body reacts.
Sends out stem cells.
They go to the cut.
Make new skin.
The cut heals.

Scraped arm

Stem cells healed
the scrape

A person may be sick.
She may have a bad heart.
Stem cells could help.
They might even fix it.
But it would take many cells.
More than we have.
What can doctors do?
They can clone the cells.

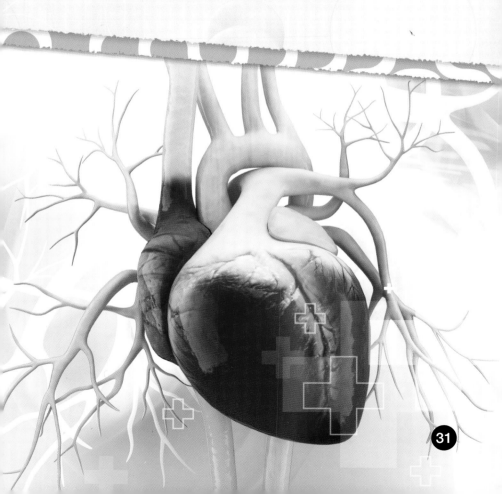

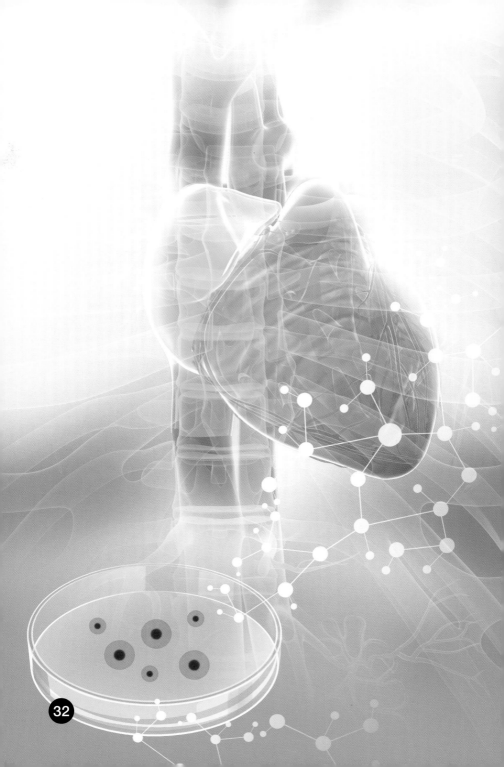

Can that happen?

Doctors are trying.

They are using heart stem cells.

Copying them.

They put them in people.

People with bad hearts.

It helps the hearts heal.

Doctors hope to do more.

Stem cells could do a lot.

Grow new *organs*.

Heal hurt ones.

DO YOU COPY?

99 percent of everyone's genes are the same.

Chapter 7
HELPING THE SICK

Doctors want to know more.
They study genes.
Do tests.

There are *risks*.
So they can't test people.
It is not safe.
But they can test animals.
Like mice.
They are easy to work with.
Mice grow fast.
Their genes are like ours.

DO YOU COPY?

90 percent of human genes are found in mice.

Not all mice are alike.

Some are big.

Others are small.

Some are gray.

Or white.

They can be healthy.

Or sick.

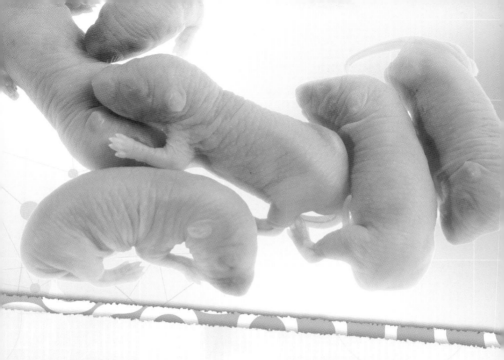

Scientists want mice that are the same.

It helps with tests.

They need identical mice.

Today they can get them.

How?

They clone them.

The cloned mice are tested.

We find out what is good for mice.

And what is bad.

We learn.

The same things may be good for us.

Or bad.

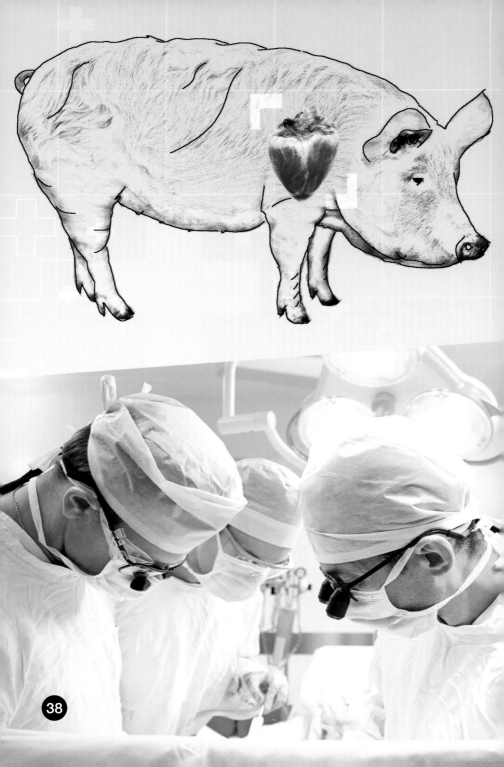

Cloning can do more.
Some people need new organs.
They need a *transplant*.
There are not enough.
People wait a long time.
Many die.

Some doctors had an idea.
They tried pig organs.
Pig organs are like ours.
Doctors put them into people.
But they were rejected.
Human bodies did not like them.

What if the organs had human genes?
They would act like human organs.
They might not be rejected.
Doctors want to find out.

Chapter 8
ANIMAL CLONES

Remember Dolly?

She was the first cloned mammal.

Soon there were more.

Mice in 1998.

Another year went by.

A bull was cloned.

People kept trying to clone animals.

Why?

Some animals are stronger than others.

Some run faster.

Some make better meat.

Or sweeter milk.

Or thicker wool.

Or lay more eggs.

They are super animals.

They have good genes.

People want more of them.

Super animals are worth a lot.

DO YOU COPY?

Scientists have created special goats. They have spider genes. The goats make spider silk in their milk. The silk is as strong as steel.

Some animals are pets.

People love them.

But pets die.

Owners are sad.

They don't want a new pet.

They want their pet back.

Some think they can get it.

How?

Cloning.

Pets are being cloned.
A cat was copied in 2001.
Four years went by.
A dog was cloned.

Cloning costs a lot of money.
But some will pay it.
They want their pets.
But there are problems.
The cloned pets share genes.
But they may not look like the old pet.
They may not act the same.
It is a risk.

Chapter 9
SHOULD WE CLONE?

The science is exciting.
It can help the sick.
Doctors learn from it.
Find cures.
Save lives.
But it is still a gamble.
We do not know a lot.

Cloning can have big risks.
Stem cells look like *cancer* cells.
They can act the same too.
Divide a stem cell.
Do it over and over.
The cells may turn into cancer cells.
That is what some think.

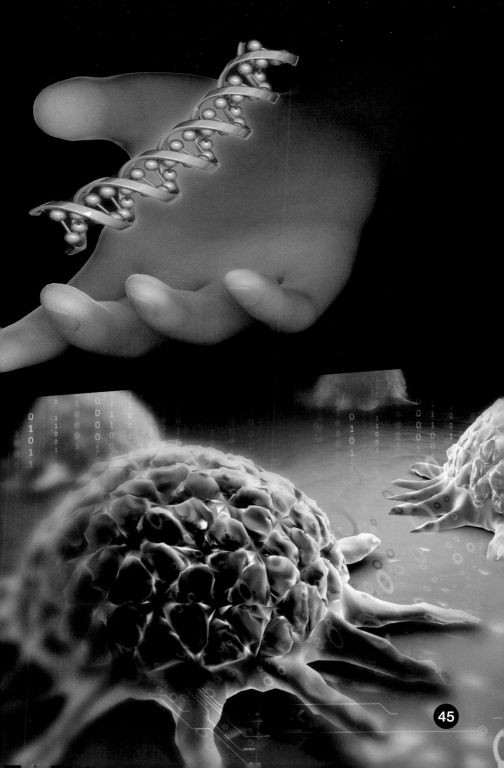

Many *religions* don't like cloning.
There are strong feelings.
It is like making life.
Many feel that is wrong.

Others worry about the risks.
What if a country clones people?
Uses them to fight.
Like soldiers.
Or makes them slaves.

DO YOU COPY?

A Korean scientist said he cloned a human in 2002. He lied. It was a hoax.

Chapter 10
WHAT'S NEXT?

Cloning can save animals.
Some may become *extinct*.
It could keep them alive.
Like pandas.
And rare tigers.

It can do a lot of good.
But some worry.
There are still many risks.
Things we don't know.

No one has the answers.
Doctors don't know enough.
So laws have been passed.
Everyone agrees.
No one will clone people.
For now.

Research goes on
Doctors find new uses each year.
Healthier animals.
Better food.
Cures for diseases.
New body parts.
Organs that heal.
It is good to learn.

But it can also be scary.
We don't know what will happen.
The only way to know is to test.
There are many dangers.

Clones could save us.
Or end us.
It's all in how they are used.
What's next for clones?
You will help decide.

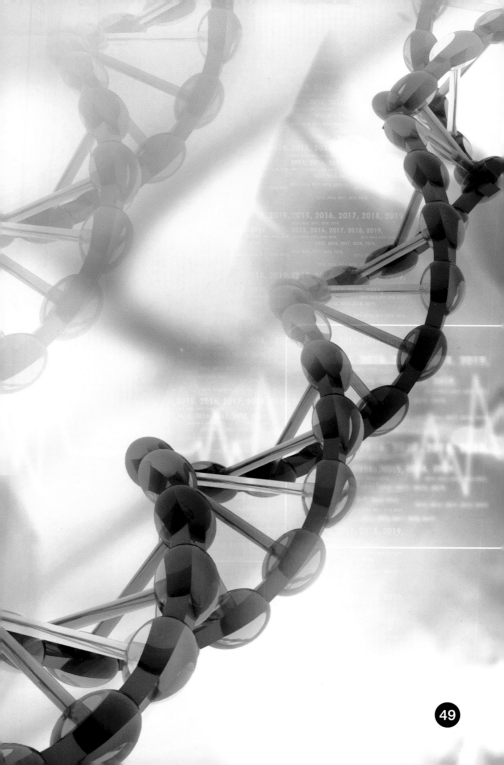

GLOSSARY

cancer: a disease caused by abnormal cells

cell: the smallest thing that makes up a plant or animal

clone: a cell, plant, or animal that is a copy

DNA: deoxyribonucleic acid; a substance in cells that controls how plants and animals grow

embryo: unborn baby in the first days or weeks of growth

extinct: to have died out

genes: parts of a cell that control how a person looks and grows

identical: exactly the same

mammal: an animal that feeds milk to its babies and usually has hair or fur

natural: not made by people

nucleus: the middle part of a cell that holds the DNA

organ: a part of the body that helps the body in some way

religion: a system of beliefs used to worship a god

risk: a chance that something bad will happen

somatic cell: a cell that helps form the body

stem cells: simple cells in the body that can become any other kind of cells

tissue: the material that makes up parts of a plant or animal

transfer: to move from one living thing to another

transplant: to place an organ from one person into another person

twinning: a way to clone by splitting an embryo in two

TAKE A LOOK INSIDE

VIRTUAL REALITY

Many companies have hologram devices.
Sony makes one.
Put it on.
Shine light on a cartoon robot.
The robot will close its eyes.

Microsoft has a tinted *visor*.
It puts holograms on top of
the real world.
A VR glass on a real table.
A VR monster in your bedroom.
Fantasies become real.
You can it use for work.
Or for fun.

THAT'S COOL
Scientists want to use a
hologram visor to explore
Mars.

How does this work?
HMDs have two screens.
One for each eye.
This tricks a person's eyes.
They think they are seeing things for real.
But it's all virtual.

VR has taken off since then.
People are testing new tools.
Joysticks.
A *mouse*.
Even gloves.

Chapter 2
THE SOMETIMES REAL WORLD

Virtual reality.
VR for short.
It seems real.
But it is created by computers.
Why does it seem real?
It has three *dimensions*.

Height.
Width.
Depth.
Just like the real world.

You can play in the virtual world.
Work.
Take trips.
Meet new people.
You can try new things.
Fly a jet.
Race a car.
Walk on Mars.
Hold a person's heart in your hand.

red rhino b👓👓ks®

NONFICTION

9781680210316

BIOWEAPONS
LESLIE BUTEYN
9781680210729

CANNIBAL ANIMALS
JOHN PERRITANO
9781680210484

CLONING
SUSAN HENNEBERG
9781680210347

COMET CATCHER
JOHN PERRITANO
9781680210477

DRONES
SUSAN HENNEBERG
9781680210293

FAULT LINES
JOHN PERRITANO
9781680210538

GNARLY SPORTS INJURIES
JOHN PERRITANO
9781680210712

GREAT SPIES of the WORLD
JOHN PERRITANO
9781680210491

HACKED
M.G. HIGGINS
9781680210378

LITTLE ROCK NINE
JOHN PERRITANO
9781680210552

MEDAL OF HONOR
JOHN PERRITANO
9781680210545